Family Favorites From Moonlite®

RECIPES THAT FOUNDED
A KENTUCKY TRADITION

®2005 by Moonlite Bar-B-Q Inn, Inc.
2840 West Parrish Avenue
Owensboro, Kentucky 42301
Visit our website: www.moonlite.com

Library of Congress Control Number: 2005922416
ISBN: 0-9766896-0-X

Printed and Published in the United States of America.

Publisher: Moonlite Bar-B-Q Inn, Inc.
Editor: Patrick Bosley
Food Editor & Stylist: Moretta Bosley
Food Photography: Patrick Bosley
Graphic Design: Wiesenberg Design Studio, Inc.

Contents

Welcome...

The Bosley's hope you enjoy our cookbook. We have been serving Hickory Smoked Bar-B-Q for over 40 years, taking pride in being one of Kentucky's finest restaurants, with three generations of Bosley's to serve you.

The Bosley family in 1975. This marks the transition from a 30 seat diner to the restaurant you know today.

If you are in the Owensboro, Kentucky area stop by, there is always a family member working. We are open from 9:00 a.m. to 9:00 p.m. Monday through Thursday, from 9:00 a.m. to 9:30 p.m. on Friday and Saturday, and from 10:00 a.m. to 3:00 p.m. on Sunday. We are closed every Sunday night as well as all day Easter Sunday, Thanksgiving Day, Christmas Day, and New Years Day in order to spend time with our families.

Order from our extensive menu, or fill up at our famous buffet (see page 6 for buffet times). Our buffet features a changing variety of delicious **Bar-B-Q'd mutton, pork, ribs, chicken, smoked ham,** and **beef.** We also have country ham, homestyle vegetables, a fantastic salad bar and a dessert bar featuring our own pies and other desserts.

Moonlite Famous for Bar-B-Q

The restaurant is just part of its business enterprise that requires the services of the second generation Bosley family — Hugh Jr., Ken, Fred and Janet — as well as several of the third generation and over 100 more employees.

Along with our restaurant and take out service, Moonlite Bar-B-Q also has a renowned catering department, a wholesale foods division, a complete restaurant equipment company, an international website, and don't forget our mail-order to fill barbecue cravings far and wide.

Moonlite has been featured in numerous books and publications including, *Southern Living, The New Yorker,* the *New York Times* and the *Washington Post* to name a few. Check out the most recent articles below.

Ken Bosley, co-owner of Moonlite Bar-B-Q standing in front of the restaurant, is one of the four Bosleys who direct the operations of the Moonlite.

USA Today — April 2001

On April 20, 2001 the **USA Today** listed Moonlite Bar-B-Q Inn as one of the 10 great places to fill up your plate. The **USA Today** again featured the Moonlite on June 15, 2001 when it rated the Moonlite among the best barbecue in America.

Gourmet — November 2003

Gourmet Magazine's *A Guide to America's Best Roadfood* states: "Western Kentucky is a nexus of great barbecue, and Moonlite is its shining star. Help yourself to brisket, ribs and mutton, plus the hunter's stew known as burgoo. A sign at the buffet warns *Not Responsible for Your Overeating.*"

Southern Living — 2003

Southern Living *Bar-B-Que Our Ultimate Guide* lists Moonlite Bar-B-Q Inn among the South's Best Restaurants. "A once-plentiful but now-vanished local resource — sheep — has given Owensboro, Kentucky a special place in the world of barbecue."

"Moonlite Bar-B-Q Inn, the biggest of the local barbecue joints, serves 10,000 pounds of mutton a week, counting the 325-seat restaurant, the catering sideline, and the growing mail-order business. Ken Bosley, whose family owns the restaurant, describes the taste as being "like an excellent piece of aged beef."

Moonlite Buffet

Menu Service

The Campbell family dine together at the Moonlite

Blue Ribbon Desserts

Carry Out

Bud Bush serves Mike Roby in Moonlite's Carry out

According to *Gourmet Magazine* Moonlite's famous buffet is "spectacular" and "Puts Owensboro barbecue in a class by itself." That's nothing new for Moonlite. People come from miles around to feast on their world famous buffet. It is not uncommon to see people from all over the world, from Russian Goodwill Ambassadors, to bus loads from New Zealand, Moonlite is always a must stop for anyone visiting from out-of-state, or from out of the country. The buffet is contained in it's own room, with staff that keeps the contents fresh, clean and never ending. On one side of the buffet there is an abundance of barbecue and other meats with a large collection of country style vegetables including our special recipe *Corn Muffins.* Along with a large salad bar located across the room that features our own recipe for *Banana Salad,* our *Blue Ribbon Desserts* have their own counter and you can always find a warm cobbler and soft serve ice cream.

The lunch buffet is served from 11:00 a.m. to 2:00 p.m., Monday thru Saturday. A dinner buffet is served from 4:00 p.m. to 9:00 p.m., Monday thru Thursday, and 3:30 p.m. to 9:30 p.m. on Friday and Saturday. On Sunday a brunch buffet is served from 10:00 a.m. to 2:30 p.m., and the restaurant closes at 3:00 p.m. on Sunday so the family can spend some time together.

Along with the buffet, the restaurant features a menu of Barbecue dinners, sandwiches, country ham, deliciously seasoned vegetables, fresh salads, (catfish on Thursday and Friday nights), and homemade deserts including some of their blue ribbon pies.

Moonlite also has a fast-paced carry out department which serves the Owensboro area with a complete take out menu. We offer everything from sandwiches to by the pound products in our take out. You can also choose from a large selection of canned and bottled products, T-shirts, hats, cookbooks and a wide selection of speciality items.

Mail Order

We offer some of our most requested products by mail order as a service to our customers. You can request a free mail order catalog by writing:

Catalog Request
Moonlite Bar-B-Q Inn
2840 W. Parrish Ave
Owensboro, Ky. 42301

Sliced Country Ham, Moonlite Burgoo and Rebecca Ruth Candies being packaged in bubble wrap for shipping.

Order Information

Place your order on the Internet at www.moonlite.com
or call any weekday 9 a.m. to 4 p.m. Central Time
Toll Free: 1-800-322-8989 Orders only please.
Phone: 270-684-8143 • Fax: 270-684-8105

Website

Our Website started around 1996 as a college project by Pat Bosley, third generation family member, and David Hanna a college friend and fraternity brother. Moonlite's website started long before e-commerce sites became popular. The idea was sold to Moonlite because Pat, David and their friends were willing to work for food. The URL *moonlite.com* was later registered in July 1997.

Visit our website at **www.moonlite.com** to order our products on-line anytime, or for additional information on our restaurant, upcoming events, and specials. Be sure to visit us often since we are always up-dating our website to better serve you our customers.

The Moonlite Bar-B-Q Tradition:
Barbequing for over 40 years

Moonlite Bar-B-Q began in the mid 1940's... by the 50's Sonny & Sadie Bertram and J.C. & Betty Stinson, had made *Moonlite* into a popular local Bar-B-Q establishment. In February 1963, Hugh and Catherine Bosley sold their house, using the $5,000 profit to make the down payment, and bought *Moonlite* for $50,000.

With no place to live, they moved in with Catherine's mother and entered the restaurant business with no experience and little formal education. At that time the *Moonlite* was a fourteen year old barbecue joint with 30 seats including stools at the counter. He was 48, she was 42 and they had five children. Pappy drove a cab for Veterans Cab Company and worked at Fleischmans Distillery. Catherine was a foreman

Hugh "Pappy," Bosley Sr. (1914 – 2003)
Catherine Bosley, (1919 – 2003)

at Glennmore Distillery. It was Pappy's layoff from Fleischmans that caused them to re-examine their opportunities, leading to the purchase of the Moonlite. Their five children grew up working next door to the *Moonlite* at the Big Dipper (a local hamburger establishment.)

Over the last 40 plus years, *Moonlite Bar-B-Q* has grown into a very special business. In this time of chain stores and merged companies, *Moonlite* has grown as a family business with children and grandchildren working together to keep things going and growing.

Moonlite now requires a staff of over 120 dedicated members working various

Moonlite's current entrance has been in use since 1979, as a result of the widening of Parrish Ave.

Pappy teaching the third generation, grandson Mike to cook barbecue Mutton.

Catherine working the Moonlite Counter.

facets of the business. These areas now include a 350 seat restaurant with a busy carry out and gift department, a USDA inspected processing plant, an extensive Catering department (capable of serving 15 to 15,000 with unparalleled quality and professionalism), a Wholesale division serving the region with barbeque and related products through distributors in a four state area. All this from a 30 seat roadside restaurant in 1963.

Catherine had kept her job at Glennmore until retiring just in case the restaurant didn't make it. Before she passed away in 2003 claimed, "The *Moonlite* just might make it… we should keep our options open just in case."

Moonlite Catering

If you don't want to take some home with you, or have it mailed, you can have the Moonlite's special fare come to you! Moonlite's catering department handles anything from a picnic basket for the family outing, to black tie affairs, weddings and company picnics. They have catered company picnics for over 15,000, and traveled as far away as California.

Our professional staff can make the arrangements, prepare the food, and then provide the service at your home, office, or wherever you choose.

Be sure to schedule your catering events early!

Hugh "Benny" Bosley, Jr., Moretta Bosley, and Jeanie Bosley Heath catering for the City Meals on Wheels Great American and French Chefs Barbeque Challenge in New York City.

Left: Catering a formal dinner party at the River Park Center in Owensboro, Kentucky.

Above: Behind the scenes while catering a large outdoor company picnic.

Left: Catering a company picnic of about 15,000 people.

Moonlite's Wholesale Foods

In 1983 due to expanding sales beyond our restaurant to other restaurants, groceries and gift shops around the country we applied for and received United States Department of Agriculture approval. Following USDA guidelines insures Moonlite has top quality products on the market.

A major operation behind the scenes at Moonlite, that most people never see or hear much about, is the USDA inspected processing plant which provides

the wholesale division USDA inspected meats and products to sell to restaurants, schools and grocery stores. Moonlite delivers these products in their own delivery trucks, and also uses distributors like Tree of Life M.W., Kehe Foods Dist., Clark Restaurant Services, and Davis Distributors. Look for Moonlite products in Louisville, Paducah, Evansville, Bowling Green, or your local Wal-Mart Grocer. Moonlite products are distributed far and wide, so you never know where Moonlite will show up next.

Perry Howard trims sheep to be quartered for cooking or sales to wholesale customers.

Bosley Equipment

Bosley Equipment Company is a division of Moonlite which develops and markets new and used restaurant equipment. In fact, the special equipment used in the Moonlite operation was designed and built by Hugh, Jr.

Bosley Equipment sales, installs and maintains equipment in other restaurants and institutional kitchens throughout the area.

Hugh "Benny" Bosley, Jr. is in charge of the Equipment Company a division of Moonlite.

A Little Background About Our Products

Our Bar-B-Q is slow cooked over a *Hickory log fire in our custom built pits.* This method of cooking imparts a distinctive flavor to our beef, chicken, mutton, pork, and ribs.

Real Bar-B-Q, according to government standards, must be cooked to lose at least 30% of its original weight. This can be done in many ways, but the only way we do it is with our slow cook method, our pit cooks dip (baste) each piece several times during the process. We don't even put sauce on our meats until after it's cooked.

Our meats are slow cooked over a hickory log fire and basted with our vinegar based pit dip. This imparts the flavor that Moonlite is famous for.

Most places are afraid to let their Bar-B-Q be tasted unless its swimming in sauce. (At the restaurant, you put the sauce on at the table.)

Our Burgoo is a thick hearty soup made with lots of mutton, beef, chicken, and vegetables. It is the perfect accompaniment with Bar-B-Q that has its roots far back in time. In this part of the country, early settlers made a stew that consisted of any meats and vegetables available. That often meant game meat such as deer, squirrel, raccoon, rabbit or quail. As time passed, each cook fine tuned his or her recipe by adding special ingredients that made their Burgoo the "best". Burgoo is a traditional menu item at historic racetracks such as Churchill Downs and Keeneland. The first Saturday in May, cooks all around Kentucky get started on this Derby Day Tradition. Burgoo is part of the Church Picnic Fare in all of Western Kentucky throughout the summer.

Plan to come to Owensboro the second weekend in May to experience the best Burgoo and Bar-B-Q in the world with 60,000 of your newest friends at The International Bar-B-Q Festival, truly a sight you must see to believe.

Remember, when you are visiting Owensboro: **"The Bar-B-Q Capital of The World,"** don't forget to stop by to say hi!

Burgoo and Thoroughbred racing are very popular in Kentucky.

A little trivia: "Kentucky Burgoo" is the celebrated stew which is served in Kentucky on Derby Day, at Political Rallies, Horse Sales and other outdoor events. Mr. J. T. Looney, of Lexington, is one of Kentucky's most famous Burgoo-makers and it was for him that Mr. E. R. Bradley named his 1932 Kentucky Derby winner "Burgoo King". The blanket of roses designed in 1931, by Mrs. Kingsley Walker for the Kentucky Derby winner was first worn in 1932 by "Burgoo King".

12

The Burgoo Story

Owensboro's burgoo is a hearty soup made from mutton, chicken, and a variety of vegetables. No two cooks prepare it the same way and most keep their recipes a closely guarded secret.

One tradition says that burgoo came to this country from Wales. It found it's way to the Kentucky frontier through Virginia, but Daviess Countians have long claimed that the Welsh-Virginian dish was a low quality soup, not burgoo.

The evolution of burgoo, and its contents in its early days, seem markedly similar to those of Brunswick Stew. Burgoo developed in the early 1800's as a squirrel stew with vegetables and it was first served to crowds at political rallies and later at church picnics.

Burgoo experts disagree about what meats actually go into burgoo. Each area of Kentucky, and even individual burgoo cooks use different types of meat in their burgoo. At the Moonlite Bar-B-Q Inn we prefer to use mutton, beef, and chicken. Mutton gives burgoo a wild game like flavor that holds its own against the red pepper and vegetables in our burgoo. Mutton gives the burgoo the same oomph that squirrel and other wild game formerly provided.

About the only point on which burgoo experts agree is the consistency of the soup. A good burgoo should be thick, but still soupy. This is the reason for the long, slow cooking time. It gives the burgoo time to thicken naturally.

Owensboro/Daviess County
Barbecue Capitol Of The World

Owensboro Riverfront, photo courtesy of Charles Mahlinger.

"A Pit Above The Rest" — If It's Not Owensboro Barbecue, It's Not Real Barbecue.

Owensboro, known early in its history as Yellow Banks, is named for Col. Abraham Owen, a Kentucky legislator and soldier. Owensboro is the county seat of Daviess County, named for soldier-lawyer-orator Col. Joseph Hamilton Daveiss (the "i" and "e" in Daveiss' name were accidentally switched in the legislation creating the county's name.

Owensboro commands a sweeping view of the Ohio River from its downtown river front. The historic river helped give birth to the city nearly two centuries ago and nurtured its growth by bringing steamboats laden with passengers and goods to the city's doorstep.

Among other things, Owensboro is famous for the International Bar-B-Q Festival, which draws barbecue fans from all over the world. The Festival held the second weekend each May, helped put Owensboro on the map. Every May 20,000 pounds of ewes (female sheep, known as mutton) are cooked over open pits fired by hickory

Moonlite Bar-B-Q Booth at the International Bar-B-Q Festival.

14

logs. Different teams of area barbecue cooks compete to see who has the best mutton, chicken and burgoo.

Daviess County comes by its claim to barbecue fame naturally. The first barbecue on record here, but probably not the first in county history, was on July 4, 1834. Since then the barbecue fires have been burning almost continuously from summer to summer. Some families are now on their fifth generations of barbecue cooks. Each summer parish barbecues attract 5,000 or more people to a single picnic. In 1981 parrish cooks estimated that well over 50 tons of mutton, 10,000 chickens, and 4,000 pounds of pork were consumed along with 8,000 gallons of burgoo.

What distinguished Owensboro's barbecue from the barbecue in the rest of the world? It's the local popularity of barbecued mutton.

Yet why is barbecued mutton so popular here?

There seems to be about as many answers to that question as there are sheep roasting over the pits.

Some say that the early Welsh settlers who made Daviess County home raised enormous herds of sheep; so it was only natural that if a barbecue was in order, mutton would be the meat. Agricultural records for early Daviess County seem to support that argument. In 1860, for example, there were more than 11,000 sheep, compared to 6,570 beef cattle, obviously radically different from today's records. With packs of wild dogs ravaging the farmer's flock, sheep herding is not as popular in Daviess and surrounding counties as it once was. Instead, the mutton served in Owensboro today probably originated in Minnesota, Iowa, North Dakota or South Dakota.

Others explain the passion for barbecued mutton as an acquired taste that began with the early Roman Catholic picnics, which served mutton because it was the meat parishioners donated. If there had been an abundance of beef cattle, then it would have been beef that was barbecued.

Parallel to this explanation is the idea that mutton doesn't taste good fried or boiled. To some in those early days, barbecuing mutton was the only way that these four-legged creatures were good to eat.

Smothers Park on the Downtown Riverfront, photo courtesy of the Owensboro Tourist Commission.

Kentucky Traditions

Bar-B-Q and Kentucky Bourbon

Moonlite Bar-B-Q and Wathen's Kentucky Bourbon, a premium Kentucky Bourbon created by Charles W. Medley, both use family recipes and techniques that have been handed down unchanged through generations. Time honored tradition, hands-on expertise, and old-fashioned know-how are the ingredients that make Moonlite Bar-B-Q, and Wathen's Kentucky Bourbon two Kentucky traditions.

Local Champions

Championship basketball is nothing new to Kentucky. Everyone knows about UK Basketball. Owensboro too, is the home of champions. Kentucky Wesleyan College, division 2 has won 8 national championships! Visit www.kwc.edu for more information.

Home of Bluegrass Music

Besides, Barbecue Capital of the World, *Home of Blue Grass Music* is another label by which travelers can identify Owensboro, home of the International Bluegrass Music Association (IBMA) and Museum, You can visit their website at www.bluegrass-museum.org

Moonlite proudly contributes to Blue Grass and the arts so, tune up your banjos and fiddles. Visitors can enjoy jam sessions of top Bluegrass artists, as well as famous Daviess County barbecue at local events. Contact the Owensboro Tourist Commission for events and times: 1-800-489-1131.

Owensboro Offers A Unique NASCAR Heritage

No less than six NASCAR drivers and several pit crew members are from the Owensboro area. The drivers are: Darrell Waltrip, Michael Waltrip, Jeremy Mayfield, David Green, Jeff Green and Mark Green. Owensboro offers several well kept secrets for the NASCAR

enthusiast. Brewco Motorsports is located in Central City just 30 miles from Owensboro. They are the only Bush Series Team in Kentucky. For more information go to www.brewco.com. Owensboro also features the Speedzeum, an exhibit at the Owensboro Museum of Science and History, featuring Owensboro's racing legacy. Contact the museum at www.owensboromuseum.com.

Famous Kentucky Country Ham From Moonlite

Kentucky Country Ham is different from "conventional" ham in the following ways:

Curing Method — Curing ingredients are pumped into the conventional ham as a brine or pickle. They are applied to the country ham as a dry-rub.

Moisture Content — Water is added to the conventional ham by the curing process. The country ham, on the other hand, is shrunk 20 to 30 percent through curing and aging, and is therefore much drier.

Flavor — Country ham flavor is much more intense, due to concentration through loss of water, and enzymatic activity during aging.

This ham does not require refrigeration until you start using it. Keep it hanging in a cool dry place until ready to use. The ham must be kept away from flies and insects. **Always unwrap ham. Never store in a box.** You can prepare Kentucky Country Ham many ways baked, boiled, broiled, or fried.

Important

You may expect your Country Cured Ham to have a higher salt content than packing house type. The salt and heavy shrinkage makes the country ham keep for months, even years without refrigeration. These hams are not tenderized or precooked — just country cured, smoked, and aged. Often times white specks appear throughout the meat in aged hams. This in no way affects the quality of the meat but is preferred by many connoisseurs. Due to aging, your ham will have some mold on it. This in no way affects the quality of the meat, but rather indicates proper aging. Wash whole hams thoroughly, use just plain water and clean cloth.

Notes: Some things Grandmother Osborne taught us:

1. When planning a party figure on 3 to 5 bite size appetizers per person per hour.

2. You can substitute yogurt for cream cheese.

Appetizers, Snacks and Pickles

Appetizers, Snacks and Pickles

Moonlite's Ham and Cheese Ball, page 22

EASY BREAD & BUTTER PICKLES
Aunt Nancy Tongate

25 – 30 cucumbers (squash, etc...) sliced thin
8 large onions, sliced
½ cup salt, sprinkled on above

Sprinkle salt over cucumbers and onion slices and let stand for 3 hours. Drain.

5 cups sugar
5 cups cider vinegar
1 teaspoon Turmeric
½ teaspoon cloves
1 teaspoon celery seed

Combine sugar, vinegar, Turmeric, cloves and celery seed in a large pot, and bring to a boil. Place cucumbers in jar, cover with the hot liquid and seal.

Variation: You can also add peppers, squash, zucchini or green beans, etc...

Chris Bosley makes these pickles every year from cucumbers out of Pappy's garden.

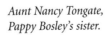

Aunt Nancy Tongate, Pappy Bosley's sister.

AUNT NANCY'S PICKLED PEACHES

6 pounds Cling Peaches
6 cups sugar
2 cups water
2 cups vinegar white
2 ounces pickling spice tied in cloth bag

Peel peaches, place in large pot; add sugar, water vinegar and spice bag. Bring to a boil and cook for 5 minutes until tender. Let stand in syrup overnight. Remove peaches and place in jars. Cook syrup 8 – 10 minutes (until it comes to a rolling boil) and pour over peaches in jars. Cap while syrup is still hot.

SUE BOSLEY'S SNACKIES

1 pound ground beef
1 pound sausage
1 pound Velveeta® cheese
Salt and pepper to taste
¼ teaspoon oregano
2 small packages small party rye bread

Cook ground beef and sausage together in skillet and drain. stir in cheese until all is melted. Add oregano.

Spread this mixture onto the rye bread. Can be frozen before baking. Heat in 350° oven until slightly brown and hot through, about 10 – 15 minutes.

Sweet-n-Sour Meatballs

2 pounds ground beef
1 medium onion, chopped
3 jars grape jelly
2 jars chili sauce
Juice of one lemon

Mix ground beef and onion. Form into small meatballs. Refrigerate until needed.

Bring grape jelly, chili sauce, and lemon juice to a boil. Drop meatballs into the mixture and cook about 5 minutes. Serve warm.

Refrigerate leftover sauce for later use. Spoon off grease as it sets on top. Leftover sauce may be frozen.

Moonlite Ham & Cheese Ball

8 ounces chopped ham
16 ounces cream cheese
2 teaspoons Accent®
2 teaspoons Worcestershire sauce
1 tablespoon instant minced onion
1 cup chopped pecans – to roll ball in

Mix all ingredients well, shape into ball and roll in chopped pecans. This makes one small cheese ball. Double the recipe for one large cheese ball.

Since Moonlite's hams are cooked on open pits over hickory wood they have a subtle smoked flavor that really enhances this cheese ball recipe.

SHRIMP MOUSSE

1 can tomato soup

1 (8 ounce) package cream cheese

2 envelopes plain gelatin, softened for 5 minutes in
½ cup water

2 small cans shrimp pieces

¼ cup green onions, diced

¼ cup green peppers, diced

1 cup celery, diced

¼ teaspoon each: salt, pepper, celery salt, onion salt

Dash of hot sauce

1 cup mayonnaise

2 tablespoons horseradish, drained

Heat soup and cream cheese. Stir with a wire whisk until cheese is melted. Some small lumps will remain. Add dissolved gelatin to hot soup and cheese mixture. Remove from heat and stir well. Add remaining ingredients. Pour into well greased 1-quart mold (we use a fish mold). Refrigerate. Unmold and serve as an appetizer spread with assorted crackers.

A Catering Department favorite!

BEEF ROLL-UPS

¾ cups Hellmann's® Mayonnaise
1 heaping teaspoon horseradish
Cooked beef, sliced thin
  (Moonlite's barbecued beef is excellent)
Sesame bread sticks

Mix horseradish and mayonnaise. Spread the mixture onto beef slices. Roll around each bread stick. Cut roll-ups into 1½ inch lengths.

CURRY DIP

2 teaspoons curry powder
2 teaspoons seasoned salt
1 teaspoon dill weed
1 tablespoon parsley flakes
1 tablespoon dried chives
1 cup Hellmann's® Mayonnaise
1 cup sour cream

Mix all ingredients together, chill and serve with raw vegetables such as: cauliflower, celery, cherry tomatoes, cucumbers, green peppers, carrot sticks, broccoli, radishes, squash.

Yield: 2 cups

The curry dip is one of the favorites from our Catering Department. This is a great dip to serve with chips. We have also used it as a sandwich spread.

Stuffed Mushroom Caps

Filling For Approximately 200 Mushroom Caps

Beef Filling – mix together:

2½ pounds dried beef (shredded)
2 pounds cream cheese (softened)
3 pints sour cream
1 cup mayonnaise (not salad dressing)
¼ cup minced onion
3 tablespoons parsley flakes
2 tablespoons Beaumonde seasoning
2½ tablespoons dill weed

Shrimp Filling – mix together:

2 pounds cream cheese
1½ pounds minced shrimp pieces
1 pint mayonnaise
1 ounce minced onion
½ teaspoon garlic powder
1 teaspoon tabasco sauce
1 teaspoon Worcestershire sauce
1 teaspoon lemon juice

Cheese Filling – mix together:

2 pounds cream cheese (softened)
1 pound Velveeta® cheese (softened)
½ cup sour cream
½ ounce dry sherry
1 teaspoon celery salt

Chicken Filling – purée our chicken salad

Wash and de-stem mushroom caps, drain well. Spoon filling of your choice into caps and bake at 350° for 15 minutes or until hot all the way through. Extra mushroom stuffing can be frozen.

MARINATED MUSHROOMS

2 pounds fresh mushrooms
½ cup vinegar
¼ cup ketchup
½ teaspoon pepper
2 bay leaves
1 large red onion, sliced thin
¼ cup sugar
1 cup oil
1 teaspoon salt
2 cloves garlic
Pinch of thyme
½ cup water

Clean the mushrooms. Wipe with a damp cloth or paper towel. Put water in a sauce pan and bring to boil. Add mushrooms cover and simmer for 5 minutes. Drain thoroughly. Mix all ingredients in a large container. Add mushrooms. Cover and refrigerate. Marinate overnight, they are good for a few weeks.

Appetizers, Snacks and Pickles

QUICHE

½ pound ground beef
½ cup onion, chopped
½ cup milk
Salt
Pepper
¼ teaspoon oregano
3 eggs, beaten
1½ cups cheese, grated
½ cup mayonnaise
1 pie crust, unbaked
1 small can sliced mushrooms, optional
½ cup green peppers, chopped, optional

Brown ground beef and onion. drain. Mix together seasonings, milk and mayonnaise. Stir in eggs. Add ground beef, onions and cheese. Pour into pie crust. Bake at 375° for 30 minutes. Let stand for 5 minutes before serving.

This Quiche is good left over, refrigerate or freeze and warm in the microwave or oven.

Pie Crust: see page 121

Notes: Some things Grandmother Osborne taught us:

1. 1 cup buttermilk can be made by adding 1 tablespoon white vinegar to 1 cup of milk.

2. 7/8 cup lard equals 1 cup vegetable shortening.

3. If you don't have ½ cup packed brown sugar, you can substitute ½ cup granulated sugar and 1 tablespoon corn starch and 2 tablespoons of Molasses or Dark Corn syrup.

Breads

Biscuits, page 31

ANGEL BISCUITS

5 cups all purpose flour

¾ cup lard

1 teaspoon salt

3 teaspoons baking powder

3 tablespoons sugar

1 yeast cake dissolved in ½ cup warm water or 1 package
  dry yeast

2 cups buttermilk

Mix shortening into at least 3 cups of flour by cutting in with a fork or mixing with fingers until grumbly. Add remaining ingredients, working in the remaining flour to a soft dough. Roll out the dough and cut with a biscuit cutter. Bake at 450° for 12 to 15 minutes, or place the dough in the refrigerator and remove as needed.

Yield: 3 dozen biscuits

This is a very old family recipe. To update it you can substitute ⅞ cup vegetable shortening for ¾ cup of lard.

The third generation of Bosleys with their grandparents:
Michael, Patrick, Paul, Catherine, "Pappy", Jeanie, Gilbert and Vickie.
Not shown: Chris, Lisa, Rob, Annette and Christie.

BISCUITS

Photograph on page 29

2 cups self-rising flour
½ cup shortening
1 cup buttermilk (sweet milk may be used)
Pinch of baking powder
¼ cup powdered sugar

Mix dry ingredients together. Mix shortening into flour by cutting in with a fork or mixing with fingers until grumbly.

Add buttermilk all at once. Mix until mixture forms a soft moist dough. Fold onto floured surface (wax paper, paper towel or biscuit board). Knead gently until dough is no longer sticky. Roll out ½ inch thick. Cut with small biscuit cutter (an orange juice can or glass will do). Bake at 450° on a lightly greased cookie sheet about 10 to 12 minutes on middle rack so tops and bottoms will brown evenly.

Yield: 18 two-inch biscuits

CORNBREAD

It is better to make this batter up 30 minutes to one hour ahead of time so it can rise.

1½ cups milk
1½ cups buttermilk
⅔ cup Wesson Cottonseed Oil
3 eggs
⅔ cup melted butter
¼ cup sugar
1 cup self-rising flour
3 cups self-rising white cornmeal

Preheat oven to 475°. Beat eggs in large mixing bowl. Add all liquid ingredients. Mix well. Add flour, cornmeal and sugar. Mix well. Blend in melted butter.

Pour corn bread batter into a hot well greased muffin pan. Fill each muffin cup about half full – or pour into iron skillet or flat baking dish. Bake 10 minutes for muffins and 20 minutes for large iron skillet. You can also fry in a hot greased skillet like pancakes until brown on each side.

Yield: 24 muffins

It is important to pour into a very hot muffin pan. That is what makes our cornbread so crispy on the outside and moist on the inside.

Moretta's Green Tomato Bread

2 cups flour
1 teaspoon soda
1 teaspoon cinnamon
½ teaspoon salt
½ teaspoon nutmeg
2 eggs
½ cup sugar
½ cup brown sugar
½ cup oil
1 tablespoon lemon extract
1 cup grated green tomatoes, drained
1 cup nuts, chopped

Combine first five ingredients. Combine next six ingredients. Add dry ingredients to tomato mixture. Stir until moistened. Add nuts. Pour into loaf pan. Bake at 350° for 1 hour. Cool in pan for 10 minutes.

Yield: 1 loaf

Zucchini Bread

3 eggs
2 cups sugar
1 cup oil

Mix these ingredients and beat well. Then add:

1 teaspoon soda
1 teaspoon salt
3 cups plain flour
½ teaspoon baking powder
2 cups raw zucchini, peeled and grated
2 teaspoons vanilla
2 teaspoons cinnamon
1 cup nuts (if desired)

Bake in two loaf pans at 325° for 1 hour

Yield: 2 loaves.

As every gardener knows, in the summer zucchini is very plentiful. This is one way to use it so that the grandkids will eat their zucchini.

BANANA BREAD

1 cup shortening

2 cups sugar

4 eggs

2 teaspoons vanilla

½ teaspoon salt

4 cups sifted all-purpose flour

2 tablespoons buttermilk

2 teaspoons soda

8 ripe bananas, mashed

Cream shortening and sugar. Add eggs, buttermilk, bananas and vanilla. Mix in dry ingredients. Pour into 2 greased loaf pans. Bake at 350° for about 45 minutes. Lightly sprinkle the top of each loaf of bread with powdered sugar.

Yield: 2 loaves

This recipe is a great way to use up overripe bananas. We serve the banana bread on our dessert bar. For banana nut bread just add one teaspoon ground cinnamon and ½ cup chopped pecans.

CORN FRITTERS

1¼ cups self-rising flour
1 teaspoon sugar
Dash paprika
2 eggs, separated
2 cups whole kernel corn, drained
½ cup liquid from corn
Fat for frying
Powdered sugar or maple syrup

Mix flour, egg yolks, corn and juice from corn, sugar and paprika in mixing bowl. Stir well. Fold in beaten egg whites.

Drop by tablespoons into hot grease. Turn once. Fry until golden brown. Serve hot, sprinkled with powdered sugar or serve with maple syrup.

We don't know how many fritters this recipe makes. They always disappear before we can count them.

FRENCH TOAST

1½ cups milk
2 eggs, slightly beaten
½ teaspoon salt
6 slices bread

Mix eggs, milk and salt in flat shallow bowl. Dip both sides of bread into batter. Brown on lightly greased skillet or griddle. Sprinkle with powdered sugar and serve at once with syrup.

A pinch of sugar in the mixture will make it brown easier.

Yield: 6 servings

PANCAKES

1½ cups self-rising flour
1 cup milk (sweet or buttermilk – buttermilk is better)
2 eggs
¼ cup oil
1 tablespoon sugar

Mix together liquid ingredients. Add flour. Mix well and fry on lightly greased hot skillet or griddle.

Yield: 8 servings

CINNAMON TOAST

Sliced bread
Butter
Sugar
Cinnamon

Butter bread and place in flat pan. Sprinkle with sugar and cinnamon. Place under broiler and brown top of bread. Be careful not to burn the toast – keep a watchful eye on it!

Every child loves this recipe.

Notes: Some things Grandmother Osborne taught us:

1. Use a pizza cutter and a cutting board to "chop" fresh herbs.

2. A food processor is a fast way to chop or crush nuts.

Salads and Salad Dressings

Moonlite's Banana Salad, page 40

MOONLITE'S BANANA SALAD

Photograph on page 39

12 bananas, peeled
1 cup crushed peanuts
Banana salad dressing

Slice 4 bananas, ⅛ inch thick into a bowl. Cover bananas with light layer of Banana Salad Dressing(see below). Sprinkle with layer of peanuts. Repeat layers until all bananas are used.

Yield: 20 servings

Banana Salad Dressing

1 egg yolk, beaten
½ cup sugar
2 tablespoons vinegar
½ cup Miracle Whip®

Mix first three ingredients. Bring to a boil over low heat, stirring constantly, as it sticks easily. Remove from heat and slowly add Miracle Whip®. Keep refrigerated. Will keep up to two months.

For a great shortcut — you can now purchase Banana Salad Dressing at Moonlite's Carry Out.

CHICKEN SALAD

4 pounds boneless chicken breasts (after cooking)
4 cups chopped celery
1 teaspoon celery salt
1 heaping teaspoon white pepper
3 cups Miracle Whip®
1 healthy pinch of sugar

Slice chicken. Dice slices into large chunks. Add remaining ingredients. Add more Miracle Whip® if too dry.

Yield: 12 servings

This recipe is from Moonlite's Catering Department.

LUCILLE'S COLA SALAD

1 package Black Cherry Jell-O
1 package Strawberry Jell-O
1 (8 ounce) package cream cheese
1 (15 ounce) can seeded Bing Cherries
1 (15 ounce) can crushed pineapple
1 cup chopped nuts
2 cups Coca Cola

Drain juice from cherries and pineapple. Heat and dissolve Jell-O with juice. Cool. Mix cream cheese with 3 tablespoons Jell-O mixture. Combine pineapple, cheese and nuts. Add to Jell-O and blend well. Fold in cherries. Add cola and blend. Pour into mold. Chill until firm.

Lucille Tong is Catherine Bosley's sister. This recipe is used in our Catering Department, we like to use family recipes as much as possible.

Fruit Salad

1 (15 ounce) can white cherries
1 (15 ounce) can pineapple chunks
1 cup pecans
1 cup miniature marshmallows
1 egg
2 tablespoons flour
1 cup sugar
½ pint whipped cream

Beat egg, add juice from pineapple, flour, sugar, and cook on low heat until thick. Chill. Add remaining ingredients. Stir.

Yield: 8 servings

Cottage Cheese And Lime Jello Salad

1 (3 ounce) Package Lime Jell-O
1 cup hot water
1 cup marshmallows
1 cup cottage cheese
½ cup chopped nuts
2 teaspoons lemon juice
1 (15 ounce) can crushed pineapple
1 cup whipped cream

Dissolve Jell-O in hot water. Let cool. Mix in all other ingredients, put in loaf pan and let set in refrigerator 6 to 8 hours. Cut into squares and serve on lettuce leaf.

Garden Salad

2 tomatoes, coarsely chopped
1 cucumber, coarsely chopped
1 bell pepper, coarsely chopped
1 cup onion, chopped
1 cup vinegar
¾ cup sugar
½ teaspoon salt
½ teaspoon pepper

Mix vegetables together in large bowl. Cover with sugar, vinegar, salt and pepper. Mix well. Ready to eat or will keep a few days tightly covered in refrigerator.

Yield: 6 servings

Garden salad is good by itself and it's excellent served with dried beans.

Favorite French Dressing

1 cup sugar
⅓ cup ketchup
1 cup vinegar
1 teaspoon salt
1 teaspoon paprika
1 tablespoon chopped onion
1 cup oil
1 teaspoon celery seed

In a blender, combine sugar, ketchup, vinegar, salt, paprika, and onion. Gradually add oil. Add celery seed. Mix well and refrigerate.

Yield: 2½ cups.

SEVEN LAYER SALAD

1 cup cauliflower, chopped

1 cup celery, chopped

1 cup green onions, chopped

1 (16 ounce) package frozen green peas, thawed
and drained

1 cup mayonnaise

1 (24 ounce) package cheddar cheese, grated

7 strips bacon, fried crisp and crumbled

Olives, sliced (optional)

Place alternating layers of vegetables in bowl; spread mayonnaise over top. Cover with grated cheese and bacon. Garnish with olives, if desired. Will keep in refrigerator for about one week.

Yield: 20 servings

Variation: add 1 head lettuce, coarsely chopped as a layer.

Seven Layer Salad is another favorite among our Catering Department's customers.

MORETTA'S SPINACH SALAD

1 pound spinach, washed & torn into bite-size pieces
½ package Pepperidge Farm® Croutons
3 hard boiled eggs, sliced
⅓ to ½ pound bacon, cooked & crumbled
1 tomato, diced
1 avocado, sliced (optional)

Dressing

3 chopped green onions
1 teaspoon salt
½ teaspoon black pepper
½ cup olive oil
⅔ cup sugar
½ cup balsamic vinegar
2 teaspoons mustard

Mix dressing ingredients together and chill at least one hour. Pour over spinach and toss well. Top with croutons, egg, bacon, tomatoes and avocado.

Yield: 6 servings

Moretta serves this salad at the Bosley Family gathering every Christmas Eve.

Green Bean Salad

1 (15 ounce) can long green beans, drained
1 (8 ounce) can small peas, drained
1 (4 ounce) can pimentos, chopped & drained
½ cup chopped onion
½ cup green peppers, chopped
½ cup diced celery
1½ cups sugar
½ cup vinegar
1 teaspoon salt

Mix ingredients together. Let sit in refrigerator 6 to 12 hours before serving.

Yield: 6 servings

WATERGATE SALAD

2 (3.5 ounce) packages pistachio instant pudding mix
1 (8 ounce) small can crushed pineapple
1 (8 ounce) carton Cool Whip®
¼ cup chopped pecans
1 cup miniature marshmallows
½ cup shredded coconut

Blend pudding mix and pineapple. Add Cool Whip. Stir gently. Add remaining ingredients. Chill and serve. Garnish with a few pecans.

Yield: 6 servings

DRESSED EGGS

6 hard boiled eggs

¼ cup salad dressing
   or mayonnaise

1 teaspoon sweet pickle juice
   or ½ teaspoon vinegar

1 teaspoon sugar

½ teaspoon mustard

Pinch salt

Pinch pepper

Cut the hard boiled eggs in half. Spoon out the egg yolks and put in a bowl. Mash the yolks with a fork then add remaining ingredients. Mix well. Fill hollow egg whites with yolk mixture.

Yield: 12 Dressed Eggs

PIMENTO CHEESE

4 pounds shredded cheese
2 pounds shredded Velveeta®
2 pounds grated american cheese
2 (4 ounce) jars pimentos, chopped fine
3 cups Miracle Whip®
1 healthy pinch sugar

Mix all of the above ingredients thoroughly, mashing the cheese and Miracle Whip® together with fingers, like Grandmother does.

Yield: 8 pounds
(enough for a crowd!)

This is the recipe we use at the restaurant.

TUNA SALAD

1 (4 pound) can chunk light tuna, packed in water
1½ cups chopped sweet pickles
5 hard boiled eggs, chopped
2 cups Miracle Whip®

Drain tuna. Mix with all of the above ingredients. Add more Miracle Whip® if too dry.

Yield: 5 Pounds

This is your basic no frills tuna salad from our Catering Department. It makes a great grilled sandwich.

MACARONI SALAD

2 cups raw macaroni
1 cup mayonnaise or Miracle Whip®
2 hard boiled eggs, chopped
½ teaspoon salt and pepper – or to taste
Small package frozen peas
¼ cup pimentos, chopped
¼ cup onion, chopped
1 medium green or red bell pepper, chopped

Cook macaroni according to package directions. Drain. Rinse Macaroni well with cold water. Add remaining ingredients. Mix well. Serve cold.

Yield: 6 cups

This is the Macaroni Salad recipe we use on our buffet. We like to alternate Macaroni Salad with an Italian Rotini Salad.

Cole Slaw

1 head cabbage, medium size
½ green bell pepper
1 carrot

Trim cabbage and bell pepper, and peel carrot. Grind or shred all ingredients and stir together. Add cole slaw dressing (see below) to taste and thickness.

Yield: 8 – 10 servings

Cole Slaw Dressing

1 cup salad dressing
¼ cup sugar
2 teaspoons 100 grain vinegar
2 teaspoons water

Mix all ingredients together. Pour over cabbage mixture above.

CATHERINE'S POTATO SALAD

2 large Idaho potatoes
1 or 2 hard boiled eggs, chopped
¼ cup onion, chopped
3 small sweet pickles, chopped
½ cup Miracle Whip®
1 teaspoon vinegar
½ teaspoon salt
½ teaspoon mustard
1 teaspoon sugar

Boil potatoes until tender. Peel and cool. Cut potatoes into small chunks. Add eggs, onion, and pickle. Fold in remaining ingredients.

Yield: 4 servings

Moonlite Potato Salad

5 pounds Idaho potatoes – cook, peel, cool, chop
½ cup carrots, chopped
1 large rib of celery, chopped
¼ cup green bell pepper, chopped
1½ tablespoons sugar
1 tablespoon salt
1 medium onion, peeled and chopped
⅓ cup sweet pickle relish
4 tablespoons mustard
1 cup salad dressing

Add together ⅔ of the chopped potatoes and ½ of the chopped vegetables. Mix together the remaining potatoes and vegetables with all of the other ingredients. Stir in the potato and vegetable mixture. Mix thoroughly.

Yield: 20 servings

Moretta's Waldorf Salad

2 tablespoons orange juice
3 large tart apples, unpeeled and diced
½ cup diced celery
½ cup sour cream
½ cup raisins
¼ cup pecans
1½ teaspoons sugar

Dice apples, sprinkle orange juice over apples and toss. Combine rest of ingredients, stir well. Cover and chill. Can be made a day ahead.

Yield: 6 servings

Pappy's Wilted Lettuce Salad

3 small heads of leaf lettuce
2 hard boiled eggs
4 or 5 raw onion rings

Wash and drain leaf lettuce. Break up and put in salad bowl. Slice 2 hard boiled eggs and put on top of lettuce with 4 or 5 raw onion rings. Pour hot dressing (see below) over the salad. Serve at once.

Dressing

4 strips of bacon
1 cup sugar
1/2 cup vinegar
Salt & pepper
Bacon grease

Fry 4 strips of bacon. Crumble on top of salad. Add 1 cup sugar, ½ cup vinegar, and a pinch of salt and pepper to bacon grease. Bring to a boil. Pour over lettuce while hot, and toss.

Yield: 4 servings

Pappy Bosley was an avid gardener. He always wanted this salad made with the first lettuce of the season.

Notes: Some things Grandmother Osborne taught us:

1. Make a big pot of soup and freeze half of it. When you're in a hurry all you have to do is heat and serve.

2. Soup is a great way of using up left overs.

Soups

Moonlite's Burgoo, page 61

GRANDMOTHER OSBORNE'S BURGOO

3 quarts tomato juice

10 pounds potatoes

1½ bottles tomato ketchup

1 bottle Worcestershire sauce

1 bottle Heinz 57 Sauce

12 onions

1 head cabbage, finely chopped

2 hens

4 pounds beef

3 pounds mutton

1½ cups vinegar

4 lemons, cut in half

20 ears corn

Yield: 12 – 14 servings

This is Grandmother Osborne's recipe and ingredients, but no instructions. It is based on an early 1900's traditional recipe. We suggest you experiment and try it your way.

*Making Burgoo is an all-day affair. for a real shortcut, you can purchase Burgoo on our website at **www.moonlite.com***

Delphine with Grandmother Osborne

Moonlite's Burgoo

Photograph on page 59

4 pounds mutton
3 pounds chicken
¾ pound cabbage, ground or chopped fine
¾ pound onion, ground or chopped fine
5 pounds potatoes, peeled and diced
2 (17 ounce) cans corn (*we like Shoe Peg*)
  or 2 cups fresh corn
¾ cup tomato ketchup
3 (10¾ ounce) cans tomato purée
Juice of one lemon
¾ cup distilled vinegar
½ cup Worcestershire sauce
2½ tablespoons salt, or more to taste
2 tablespoons black pepper
1 teaspoon cayenne pepper (*more if you like*)
Add water to desired consistency

Boil mutton in enough water to cover. Cook until tender, about 2 – 3 hours. Throw out broth and bones. Chop meat fine. Set aside. Boil chicken in 2 gallons of water in large kettle until tender. Remove chicken, add potatoes, cabbage, onion, corn, ketchup and 1 gallon of water to chicken broth. Bring to a boil. Meanwhile, chop chicken meat, discard bones and skin. When potatoes are tender, add chicken, mutton, lemon, salt, pepper, Worcestershire sauce, vinegar and puree. Let this simmer for 2 hours or longer, stirring occasionally as it thickens.

Yield: 3 gallons

Some area cooks add dried or lima beans, tomatoes, and a little boiled shredded beef or wild game.

VEGETABLE SOUP

2 pounds soup bones (meat and bones)
½ cup navy beans
2 large potatoes, diced
1 pound carrots, sliced round
½ large onion, chopped
2 ribs celery, diced
1 cup fresh or frozen corn
1 large can tomatoes, coarsely chopped
Salt and pepper to taste
½ gallon water

Boil meat and beans in water until tender. Add celery and onions. Cook 15 minutes. Add carrots. When carrots are tender, add potatoes. When they are done, add corn and tomatoes.

Ready any time but best when simmered a while.

Yield: 1 gallon

Moonlite's Bean Soup

2 cups navy beans
¼ cup onions, chopped
¼ cup celery, chopped
¼ cup carrots, chopped
1 small can tomato purée
Pinch pepper and pinch salt
1 cup chopped ham or ham bone
12 cups water

Wash and soak beans overnight. Put beans into 4 qt. Kettle. Fill kettle half full of water, about 12 cups. Cook with ham until beans are almost soft. Add everything but purée. Add a little more water if beans boil dry. When the vegetables and beans are tender add the purée. Boil 1 minute. Soup is ready.

Yield: About 3 quarts

Notes: Some things Grandmother Osborne taught us:

1. 1 cup of breadcrumbs is three slices of bread that have been left out to dry, then processed in a food processor.

2. Grandmother liked using white pepper in many recipes. It eliminates the black specks and the kids won't know it's there.

3. A slice of apple in your brown sugar will keep the sugar soft.

Vegetables and Side Dishes

BROCCOLI CASSEROLE

2 packages frozen chopped broccoli
1 large onion, chopped
2 cans cream of mushroom soup
½ stick butter
½ cup bread crumbs (or croutons will be fine)
2 cups shredded Cheddar cheese
1 can mushrooms, sliced, drained
½ cup almonds, chopped

Sauté onions in butter. When onion is tender, stir in frozen broccoli. Cook a few more minutes. Add soup, mushrooms, bread crumbs and cheese. Stir until cheese is melted. Add almonds, salt and pepper. Pour into casserole dish. Bake at 350° for 20 – 30 minutes.

Yield: 8 – 10 servings

This recipe is over 20 years old. We have recipe contests at our annual employee picnic and this was an employee award winner from years ago.

COPPER PENNIES

2 pounds carrots, sliced ⅛ – ¼ inches thick
1 small onion, thinly sliced
1 green pepper, cut into strips
1 (10 ounce) can tomato soup
¾ cup vinegar
⅔ cup sugar
½ teaspoon salt
1 teaspoon prepared mustard
½ cup oil
1 teaspoon Worcestershire sauce

Boil carrots until tender. Drain. Add onions and green pepper. Mix together the remaining ingredients. Add to carrot mixture. Let this set for several hours. Will keep well in the refrigerator. Drain and serve.

Variation: You can also use canned carrots, drained.

This recipe is another annual employee picnic award winner from so long ago we don't remember who submitted the recipe.

GRANDMOTHER OSBORNE'S CORN PUDDING

2 cups fresh cut corn

2 tablespoons sugar

1½ teaspoons salt (1 teaspoon may suit your taste)

3 eggs lightly beaten

2 tablespoons butter or margarine

2 cups milk

Use well filled corn; that is, scrape the milk from the cob after cutting off the corn. Heat butter and milk. Mix in the rest of the ingredients. Pour into a greased casserole dish at least 1½ quart size. Place the casserole dish in a pan filled with hot water. Bake until firm, approximately 1 hour at 350°.

To speed up cooking time, place the casserole directly in the oven and stir from the sides as the mixture begins to thicken, 2 or 3 times.

Yield: 6 – 8 servings

You can substitute 2 cups of cream style corn and 3 tablespoons corn starch instead of fresh. Of course fresh corn is much better.

Batter For Vegetables, Onion Rings, Chicken, Etc.

¼ cup cornstarch
¾ cup flour
1 teaspoon baking powder
½ Teaspoon salt
¼ teaspoon pepper
1 egg, slightly beaten
1/3 cup cold beer or 1/2 cup water

Mix together all dry ingredients. Add ½ cup water or ⅓ cup cold beer and 1 slightly beaten egg.

Herb Batter

Add 1 teaspoon basil leaves and 1 clove minced garlic to above recipe.

Glazed Carrots

1 small package frozen baby carrots
2 tablespoons butter
2 tablespoons brown sugar
½ cup water (or ¼ cup water and ¼ cup orange juice)

Put carrots in sauce pan. Add rest of ingredients, bring to a boil. Cook until liquid is reduced by half.

Yield: 4 servings

Pappy's Parsnips

Peel and slice lengthwise. Boil in water with teaspoon salt until just tender. Do not over cook. Drain. Roll slices in self-rising flour and fry in skillet with about ⅛ inch hot shortening. Brown on both sides.

An Old Country Favorite
Fried Green Tomatoes

Pappy prefers slightly ripe, turning tomatoes, more yellow than green. Slice ¼ inch thick. Dip in self-rising corn meal. Fry in skillet with about ¼ inch hot shortening until brown on both sides. Salt and pepper to taste.

Pappy Bosley

PAPPY'S POTATO CAKES

2 cups leftover mashed potatoes
2 eggs, lightly beaten
⅓ cup flour
Salt and pepper to taste

Mix together all ingredients. Shape into patties. Fry in hot, lightly greased skillet until brown on both sides.

This is a great way to use leftover mashed potatoes, we like our potato cakes for breakfast.

PAPPY'S FRIED EGGPLANT

1 medium eggplant peeled and sliced ¼ inch thick
1 egg, beaten
Self-rising flour
Salt and pepper to taste

Peel and slice 1 medium eggplant. Soak in salted water for 10 minutes. Dip in beaten egg, then in self-rising flour. Fry in skillet with about ¼ inch hot shortening until brown on both sides.

Yield: 6 – 8 servings

Moretta says, she likes this with spaghetti and marinara sauce.

COOKED CABBAGE

1 medium head cabbage
1 quart water
1 teaspoon sugar
1 teaspoon pepper
Bacon or ham to season
1 teaspoon salt

Quarter cabbage and place in water. Add bacon or ham (we prefer barbequed ham scraps). Add salt and pepper. Cook until cabbage is tender.

Yield: 6 servings

Served on the Moonlite Buffet.

JANET'S STIR FRIED CABBAGE

½ head of cabbage, cored
2 tablespoons bacon grease
2 tablespoons water
Salt and pepper

Thinly slice a half head of cabbage (cored). Heat 2 tablespoons of bacon grease in a large skillet. Add cabbage and stir. When it looks coated (kind of shiny all over), add 2 tablespoons of water and a sprinkle of salt and pepper. Cover and cook for a minute or two. Remove lid and it's ready.

If dieting, a few tablespoons of chicken broth works just as well as bacon grease.

Yield: about 4 servings

SWEET POTATOES

4 medium sweet potatoes, peeled and sliced
1 cup brown sugar
3 tablespoons butter, melted
Marshmallows

Boil sweet potatoes in salted water until tender. Drain. Place in baking dish. In a separate bowl mix together sugar and butter. Pour over sweet potatoes. Bake in oven at 400° for 15 minutes. Cover with marshmallows and brown for about 5 minutes.

Or leave off the marshmallows and pour 1 cup of cream or Pet Milk over potatoes and brown at 400°.

Yield: 6 servings

Served on Moonlite Buffet

MOONLITE'S BARBECUED BEANS

1 (21 ounce) can pork and beans
¼ cup onion, chopped
½ tablespoon brown sugar
1 teaspoon dried mustard
3 strips bacon, chopped
¼ cup Moonlite Barbecue Sauce

Cook bacon until almost done. Add onion to bacon. Cook until onion is almost done. Add mustard and barbecue sauce. Let simmer for about 5 minutes. Add brown sugar and stir constantly until done. Place beans in baking dish. Pour bean sauce over beans and stir gently. Heat beans until temperature is 180° through.

Yield: 10 servings

GREEN BEANS

Fresh green beans
Bacon or country ham
Small whole onion

Fresh picked green beans are best or you can use canned. Break and wash. Cover with water. Add cured bacon or country ham to season, salt and pepper to taste, and a small whole onion. Cook until tender.

Or to canned green beans add 1 tablespoon of bacon grease or country ham grease, a small piece of onion and salt and pepper to taste. Cook until water is cooked out.

These country style green beans are a favorite, and you can find this Green Bean recipe used on Moonlite's Buffet.

ITALIAN PINTO BEANS

1 cup pinto beans
4 cups water
3 bay leaves
1 tablespoon bacon grease
1 tablespoon cooking wine
2 cubes beef bouillon
¼ cup celery, chopped fine
¼ cup onion, chopped fine
1 tablespoon ketchup
Salt and pepper to taste

Wash beans. Soak overnight in water or cook over high heat for 30 minutes. Turn down heat. Add bay leaves, bacon grease, celery and onion. Continue cooking until beans are half way tender. Add bouillon, wine and ketchup. Cook until tender.

Yield: 6 servings

This is an old family recipe. We are not sure where the name came from.

MORETTA'S ACORN SQUASH

2 small acorn squash cut in half and seeded
4 tablespoons brown sugar
4 teaspoons butter

Place squash cut side down in baking pan and bake at 350° for one hour or until tender. Turn over and spoon in brown sugar and butter. Bake until sugar and butter is melted.

Yield: 4 servings

Baking time will vary depending on how "ripe" or green your squash is.

GRANDMOTHER OSBORNE'S FRIED SQUASH

Slice squash ⅛ inch thick. Dip in self-rising corn meal and a little flour. Fry in skillet with about ¼ inch hot shortening until brown on both sides. Salt and pepper to taste.

MOONLITE'S
MACARONI AND CHEESE

1½ cups milk
2 cups raw elbow macaroni
2 cups Velveeta® cheese, grated
8 cups water
1½ – 2 teaspoons salt
Pinch pepper (we use white pepper)
¼ cup butter

In a large saucepan, add water and salt. Bring to a boil. Add macaroni. Cook until tender. Do not over cook. Drain and rinse macaroni and put back in same pan. Add 1½ – 2 cups milk, Velveeta® Cheese and butter (more cheese if you prefer). Stir. Simmer at low heat for 5 to 10 minutes. Serve.

Yield: 8 servings (unless you're serving the grandkids.)

Fred and Catherine disagree on the perfect macaroni and cheese. The Moonlite's macaroni and cheese is a combination of their two recipes. We use white pepper instead of black pepper because the grand kids object to black specks in their macaroni and cheese.

Vegetables and Side Dishes

FRED'S MACARONI AND CHEESE

1½ cups milk
2 cups raw elbow macaroni
2 cups grated American cheese
8 cups water
1½ – 2 teaspoons salt
Pinch pepper
¼ cup butter

Add salt to water. Bring to a boil. Add macaroni. Cook until tender. Do not over cook. Drain macaroni, add butter. In a baking dish add a layer of macaroni, then a layer of cheese. Layer remaining cheese and macaroni, ending with a layer of cheese. Add 2 cups of milk, letting it seep through, but do not stir. Add pepper to taste. Bake at 350° until cheese is brown and bubbling.

Yield: 8 servings

The second generation of Bosleys:
Jerry, Fred, Kenny, Benny & Janet

Notes: You can make your sauce ahead of time... or to save time purchase Barbecue sauces and dips at the Moonlite. Visit www.moonlite.com and click on the online store.

_____

_____

_____

_____

_____

_____

_____

_____

_____

_____

_____

_____

_____

_____

_____

_____

_____

Sauces, Dips and Gravies

Cooking Dip
To dip meat on pit while cooking

3 gallons vinegar
2 gallons worcestershire
1 quart Real Lemon®
5 gallons water
2/3 cup black pepper
26 cups salt

Mix all ingredients and bring to a boil.

Moonlite's Barbecue Pork Sauce
Original Recipe

4 gallons puree
2 gallons ketchup
4 gallons cook out barbecue sauce
3 pints vinegar
1 gallon Moonlite's Mutton Dip – see page 81
2 pounds butter
4 pounds brown sugar
5 ounces red pepper
12 ounces salt
7 gallon water

Mix all ingredients and bring to a boil, then add:

2 cups clear jel (stabilizer) mixed with 2 quarts water

Stir well – let boil a few minutes more.

MOONLITE'S MUTTON DIP

Original Recipe

Dip for chop mutton and cooked sliced mutton

1 gallon water
1⅔ cups Worcestershire sauce
2½ tablespoons black pepper
⅓ cup brown sugar
1 teaspoon MSG
1 teaspoon Allspice
1 teaspoon onion salt
1 teaspoon garlic
2 tablespoons salt
2 tablespoons lemon juice
1⅔ cups vinegar

Mix all ingredients. Bring to a boil.

Yield: 1 gallon

We no longer use these recipes because we make such huge amounts of dips and sauces, that we now have our spices custom mixed instead of using individual ones. You can purchase the Moonlite Barbecue Dip and Barbecue Sauce in our Carry Out Department.

DIP FOR 400 CHICKENS

12 gallons vinegar

8 gallons Worcestershire sauce

4 gallons ketchup

40 pounds lard

8 quarts lemon juice

4 quarts red hot sauce

4 pounds black pepper

12 pounds salt

Mix all ingredients together and bring to a boil. Use 2 new mops to put the dip on the chickens. The chickens usually cook about 6 hours and are dipped about every 30 minutes.

As a fund raiser, church members cook chickens outdoors over an open pit, dipping the chickens several times during the cooking. Once done, the chickens are sold in a few short hours.

SEAFOOD SAUCE

2 cups ketchup

2 cups chili sauce

2 tablespoons horseradish

2 tablespoons A-1 Steak Sauce

2 tablespoons Worcestershire sauce

2 tablespoons powdered mustard

Mix all ingredients well with wire whip. Serve with boiled, broiled or fried shrimp.

Yield: 3 pints

PAPPY'S HOT SAUCE

4 cups Franks Red Hot Sauce
1½ cups 100 grain vinegar
1 cup crushed red peppers
2 cups cayenne
¼ cup vodka
2½ cups water

Bring hot sauce, vinegar and water to a boil. Combine crushed peppers and cayenne peppers. Add pepper and vodka. Bring to a boil again. Let simmer.

Yield: 2 quarts

It's a whole lot easier just to purchase a bottle of hot sauce from us. It keeps almost forever and a few drops go a long way. Pappy put this hot sauce on everything!

Pappy with his sister Nancy.

CATHERINE'S RED EYE GRAVY

Fry country ham. Remove ham. Over a low to medium heat, brown the remaining ham drippings. Once brown, remove excess grease. Add ½ cup water. Stir constantly, scraping the bottom of the skillet. Bring to a boil. If more color is needed, add ½ teaspoon of Kitchen Bouquet.

Pour over fried country ham and serve.

MILK GRAVY

In a skillet, heat about ½ cup fried bacon, chicken, sausage or pork chop grease. Add 1 heaping tablespoon of self-rising flour, a little at a time. Mix well. Cook over medium heat, stirring constantly, until mixture is bubbling. Add 2 cups of milk. Continue stirring until the gravy thickens. Add salt and pepper to taste. Add a little more milk if gravy becomes too thick.

The moonlite serves milk gravy on the buffet, along with fried chicken livers — a favorite combination among our regular customers.

BROWN GRAVY

In a skillet, heat about ½ cup fried steak, chicken or liver grease. Add 1 heaping tablespoon of self-rising flour, a little at a time. Mix well. Cook over medium heat, stirring constantly, until mixture is bubbling. Add 2 cups of water. Continue stirring until gravy thickens. Add salt and pepper to taste. Add a little more water if gravy becomes too thick.

About ½ teaspoon of Kitchen Bouquet will give the gravy a richer brown color.

GIBLET GRAVY

Giblets from a turkey or chicken
Water
Juice from baked turkey or chicken (pan drippings)
1 heaping teaspoon cornstarch

For giblet gravy, cover neck, liver and gizzard with water and boil until tender. Remove parts. Cut the meat off the neck and chop up the liver and gizzard. Place back in broth. Pour in remaining juice from turkey. Mix a heaping teaspoon of cornstarch and a little bit of water in a small bowl. Add to gravy. Cook until thickened.

Notes: _____

1. Any tomato based sauce will burn if the fire is too hot.

2. Save time by purchasing your barbecue sauces, meats and dips from the Moonlite. Visit www.moonlite.com and click on the online store.

Meats and Poultry

BARBECUED MUTTON

1 hindquarter of mutton
1 quart Moonlite Cooking Dip
1 quart Moonlite Mutton Dip
Salt and pepper

Boil mutton in kettle until tender. Salt and pepper to taste. Place on outside grill or under a broiler. Baste often with *Moonlite Cooking Dip* until brown and crispy on the outside. Slice or pull meat off the bone and serve with *Moonlite Mutton Dip*.

It is best to use hickory chips on outside grill. Or, dig a pit two feet deep. Cover the pit with chicken wire. Build the fire with hickory logs. Let the fire burn to hot coals. Place meat on wire. Sop with *Moonlite Cooking Dip* often until brown and crispy on the outside. If not boiled first, cook meat for about 8 hours.

Moonlite Mutton Dip recipe is on page 83.
Moonlite Cooking Dip recipe is on page 82.

Moonlite mutton is placed on the Bar-B-Q pit raw over hot hickory logs and cooked on one side 8 hours, turned and cooked another 6 hours or so, depending upon the temperature of the coals.

BARBECUED RIBS
With Moonlite Bar-B-Que Sauce

1 slab of pork ribs
Salt
Pepper
1 pint Moonlite Barbecue Sauce

Salt and pepper ribs. Uncovered, bake in oven for 1 hour at 350°, basting ribs with sauce every 10 – 15 minutes, turning once.

Or boil on top of the stove until tender. Salt and pepper. Place on an outside grill or under the broiler. Baste with sauce every few minutes until brown.

Photo by Charles Mahlinger

BARBECUED PORK

1 pork loin roast or pork shoulder roast
Salt
Pepper
Moonlite Barbecue Sauce

Salt and pepper the roast. Bake covered in the oven at 350° or cook outside on a grill using *Moonlite Hickory Chips* for about 3 hours. Baste with *Moonlite Barbecue Sauce* during cooking.

Or you can boil the pork on top of the stove until tender. Place in a baking dish. Brown in an oven at 350° or outside on the grill, basting with *Moonlite Barbecue Sauce.*

SKILLET BARBECUE PORK CHOPS
Without Moonlite Bar-B-Q Sauce

4 pork chops
¼ cup cooking fat
1 small can tomato purée
1 tablespoon vinegar
2 tablespoons sugar
1 tablespoon Worcestershire sauce
Chopped onion or bell pepper, if desired
Salt
Pepper

Place pork chops in skillet of cooking fat. Salt and pepper to taste. Cook until brown. Pour off grease. Add purée, vinegar, sugar and Worcestershire sauce. Simmer 10 minutes.

A little chopped onion or bell pepper can also be added. If so, simmer five more minutes.

Yield: 4 servings

MOONLITE'S
FRIED COUNTRY HAM

Slice a country ham about ¼ inch thick. Trim the rind off, leaving any fat around the edges. Place the ham in a skillet and cover with water. Place a lid over the skillet and cook the ham until all water is gone, turning the ham several times. If water cooks out of the ham too fast or the ham doesn't have enough fat to fry, add a little oil and brown slowly on both sides. It's good to put some outside rind and fat in the skillet with the ham. This tends to make a better red eye gravy. Do not over cook the ham or it will be hard and dry.

For Catherine Bosley's Red Eye Gravy see page 86.

Pappy Bosley in the Carry Out section of the Moonlite. Be sure to pick up some Hot Sauce!

Boiled And Baked Country Ham

Wash whole country ham thoroughly; use plain water and a clean cloth. Place on a rack in a pan and cover with water. Bring to a boil. Simmer (do not boil) until the meat thermometer registers 170°. Insert the thermometer into the center of the ham so the bulb does not touch fat or bone and the temperature scale is above the water. Cooking time is about 15 to 20 minutes per pound for whole hams. Do not over cook the ham. Remove from water. Cool.

Ham Glaze

1 cup brown sugar
3 tablespoons mustard
Pineapple slices
Maraschino cherry halves
Peppercorns, optional

Remove the skin leaving a thin layer of fat on the ham. Score the fat into one or two inch squares. Glaze the top of the ham with one cup of brown sugar mixed with three tablespoons of mustard. Place pineapple slices and cherry halves on top of the ham. Peppercorns are also a nice garnish. Bake at 400° about 20 minutes or until brown.

Barbecued Chicken

1 whole chicken
Moonlite Barbecue Sauce
Salt and pepper

Cut chicken in half. Boil until tender. Salt and pepper to taste. Place in broiler pan of an outdoor grill. Baste with *Moonlite Barbecue Sauce* every few minutes. Cook until brown.

Any tomato based sauce will burn if the fire is too hot.

Fried Chicken

1 (2½ pound) fryer chicken
Crisco
Self-rising flour
Salt and pepper

Cut fryer up. Put enough Crisco in large skillet to fill half full. Wash and drain chicken. Dip in self-rising flour. When grease sizzles, place chicken in skillet. Sprinkle lightly with salt and pepper. Cook between medium and high until brown on one side. Turn and brown other side. Turn heat down. Cover and cook slowly for about ten more minutes. Remove the top and cook a few more minutes for crispier chicken.

Meat Loaf

½ pound sausage
1½ pounds ground beef
1 (8 ounce) can tomato sauce
1 egg
1 tablespoon Worcestershire sauce
⅓ cup green pepper, chopped
1 medium onion, chopped
¾ cup cracker crumbs, finely chopped, or oatmeal
1 teaspoon salt
¼ teaspoon pepper
¼ cup ketchup

Mix all ingredients, lightly but thoroughly. Shape meat mixture into a loaf approximately 10 x 4 x 2 inches and place in an open roasting pan. Bake at 350° about 45 minutes or until brown.

Yield: 4 – 6 servings

When meat loaf is nearly done, Moretta likes to spread ¼ cup of ketchup or tomato sauce on the top of the meat loaf and cook for another 10 minutes.

EASY CHICKEN
AND DUMPLINGS

1 (3 pound) chicken
2 cans biscuits
Salt and pepper
1 teaspoon Mrs. Dash®

Optional: 1 chicken bouillon cube dissolved in the chicken broth.

Place whole chicken in kettle. Fill kettle half-full of water. Cover. Boil chicken until tender. Remove chicken. Remove meat. Discard bones and skin. Salt and pepper broth to taste. Pat out each biscuit until thin and cut each in half. Drop in boiling chicken broth. Cook over medium heat until biscuits are done – about 5 to 10 minutes. Add boned out chicken meat and serve.

Grandmother Osborne would have been scandalized if we used canned biscuits but this makes for an easy shortcut.

BAKED TURKEY AND DRESSING

1 (10 – 12 pound) turkey
2 loaves of bread toasted
1 cup celery, chopped
1 medium onion, chopped
1 tablespoon sage
3 eggs
Salt and pepper to taste

Thaw a 10 to 12 pound turkey. Remove neck, liver and gizzard, save for Giblet Gravy see page 85. Wrap turkey in heavy aluminum foil and place in roasting pan. Add 1 quart of water to the bottom of the pan. Bake 20 – 25 minutes per pound at 350°.

For dressing, toast 2 loaves of bread. Break the toasted bread into small pieces (biscuits are good too). Sauté 1 cup of chopped celery and 1 medium chopped onion. Cook until tender. Add to toasted bread. Add 1 level tablespoon sage and salt and pepper to taste. Add juice from turkey – but save some for the gravy. If bread is not good and moist, add a little hot water or melted butter or margarine. Beat 3 eggs. Add and mix well. Put in casserole dish and bake at 350° for 20 – 30 minutes or until firm.

OYSTER DRESSING

Prepare dressing as directed above. Add 1 can of cooked oyster pieces; then heat in the same manner.

Giblet Gravy page 87.

At all family gatherings, we serve one pan of plain dressing and one pan of oyster dressing.

Notes: Some things Grandmother Osborne taught us:

1. For crispy, flaky pie crusts on cream pies, let the filling cool to room temperature before pouring into the baked crusts.

2. If you don't have ½ cup packed brown sugar, you can substitute ½ cup granulated sugar and 1 tablespoon corn starch and 2 tablespoons of Molasses or Dark Corn syrup.

3. If your brown sugar has hardened, you can microwave it for a few seconds to soften it enough to measure. (Not from Grandmother Osborne, but it works.) She said add a slice of apple in your brown sugar will keep the sugar soft.

4. One tablespoon corn starch is the same as 2½ tablespoons flour.

Cakes and Pies

Chocolate Pie, page 112

MOONLITE'S CHESS CAKE

1 box Duncan Hines® Buttery Cake Mix

¼ pound butter, melted

1 egg

Mix the above until it looks like dough. Spread into oblong cake pan. Add 12 ounces of chocolate chips on top of the dough.

1 box powdered sugar

2 eggs

8 ounces cream cheese

Mix the above until creamy. Spread onto chocolate chips. Bake at 350° approximately 35 minutes.

INCREDIBLE CAKE

From a 1960 Betty Crocker advertisement

1 box Devils Food or yellow cake mix

Mix as directed on package. Set aside.

1 cup brown sugar

½ cup cocoa

2 cups hot water

In a 13 x 9 x 2 inch pan, mix together sugar, cocoa and hot water. Pour cake mixture over this. Do not stir. Bake at 350° for about 45 minutes. Serve warm with whipped cream or ice cream.

Aunt Nancy, Pappy's sister says, "A lot of little girls loved to make this cake at my house!" She was still helping out at the restaurant in her 80's.

GRANDMOTHER OSBORNE'S BUTTERMILK CAKE

½ cup lard (you can use crisco)
2 cups sugar
1 teaspoon cinnamon
½ teaspoon nutmeg
½ teaspoon cloves
½ teaspoon Allspice
2 tablespoons cocoa
2 cups buttermilk
2 teaspoons soda
3½ cups sifted flour, plain
1 cup raisins
½ – 1 cup nuts; pecans or walnuts
1 teaspoon vanilla
½ teaspoon salt

Mix lard, sugar, spices, cocoa and salt well. Add soda and buttermilk. Slowly add flour. Mix in remaining ingredients.
Bake approximately 30 minutes at 325°.

Icing

2 cups sugar
1 stick butter or margarine
2 tablespoons Karo Syrup
¾ cup Pet Milk
1 teaspoon vanilla

Mix all ingredients together in heavy saucepan. Cook over medium heat stirring constantly until mixture forms a workable ball when a small amount is dropped in a cup of cold water. Remove from heat. Add a pinch of salt and a teaspoon of vanilla. Beat with spoon until icing is cool enough to spread onto cake.

ICE BOX FRUIT CAKE

1 pound Graham Crackers, crushed

1 pound box raisins

2 cans flaked coconut

1 pound shelled pecans, chopped

1 small jar red cherries, cut in halves

2 cans Eagle Brand Milk

1 small jar green cherries, cut in halves

½ jar lemon peel

½ jar orange peel

Mix all above thoroughly, except keep enough red and green cherries in the jars to decorate cake.

Pack the mixture in one of the ingredient cardboard boxes or in a tube or use a Bundt pan buttered well. Cover and refrigerate three to fourteen days before serving.

Grandmother Osborne used the graham cracker box and Catherine used a bunt pan.

You could always find Catherine working in Moonlite's dining room at lunchtime.

UGLY DUCKLING CAKE

1 box yellow cake mix
1 (3 ounce) package vanilla instant pudding
1 (8 ounce) can fruit cocktail
4 eggs
¼ cup oil
½ cup brown sugar
½ cup nuts
½ cup coconut

Beat eggs in mixing bowl. Add oil and brown sugar. Mix well. Add cake mix and pudding mix. Beat with mixer. Gently fold in fruit cocktail, coconut, and nuts. Pour into 9 x 13 oblong cake pan. Bake at 325° for about 1 hour.

Icing

½ cup butter
½ cup sugar
½ cup Pet Milk

Melt butter. Add sugar and Pet Milk. Boil, stirring constantly for about 2 minutes. Pour over warm cake.

Moretta Bosley says "This cake is to die for. It will quickly become your family favorite!"

STRAWBERRY PIE

4 cups sugar
3¾ cups water
¾ cup cornstarch
3 tablespoons lemon juice
3 teaspoons strawberry flavoring
3 teaspoons red food coloring
¼ teaspoon yellow food coloring
3 baked pie crusts
3 pints strawberries, capped, washed and drained well

Mix sugar and cornstarch. Add 1½ cups of water. Mix well. add 2¼ cups of water. Cook over low to medium heat, stirring constantly until thick and clear. Add lemon juice, flavoring and food coloring. Cool. Pour layer of filling into baked pie crusts, then layer of strawberries, then another layer of filling. Chill. Serve with ice cream or whipped cream.

Yield: 3 pies

Pie Crust: see page 121

Grandmother's Fried Apple Pies

Fried Pie Dough

4 cups self-rising flour
1½ cups Crisco
2½ – 3 tablespoons ice water

Mix well. Turn onto wax paper. Wrap and refrigerate for 8 hours or more.

Apple Pie Filling

2 cups fresh, frozen, or canned apples
½ cup sugar
Pinch of salt
¼ teaspoon vanilla
1 tablespoon cornstarch

Mix starch and sugar together and add to cooked apples. Bring to a boil. Cool before putting into pies.

Roll dough out thin and cut into 6 inch round circles (a saucer works well as a pattern). Place apple pie filling in the center of each circle. Fold over and press ends together with finger tips or with the edge of a fork. Fry in a skillet of shortening deep enough for pies to float, but shortening does not have to cover the pies. the grease should be hot enough to sizzle. Test the grease by dropping in a small piece of dough. If the grease is too hot the pies will brown too fast and will not cook all the way through.

Brown each pie on both sides. Remove from grease and drain on paper towels. Sprinkle each with sugar and serve warm.

Yield: about 14 pies.

This was used when the restaurant was first opened. Grandmother Osborne came in every morning and made 2 to 3 dozen pies.

BUTTERMILK PIE

1 stick (¼ pound) butter
2½ cups sugar
2 heaping tablespoons flour
4 eggs
2 teaspoons vanilla
1 cup buttermilk

Cream together butter, sugar and flour. Add eggs, vanilla and buttermilk. Mix well. Pour into 2 unbaked pie crusts. Bake for 45 minutes at 350°.

Pie Crust: see page 121

Yield: 2 pies

You can find this every sunday on our buffet.

BUTTERSCOTCH PIE

3 egg yolks
1 cup dark brown sugar
2 cups milk
¼ teaspoon salt
3 tablespoons butter
1 teaspoon vanilla
⅓ cup flour

Beat egg yolks. Add sugar, flour, salt and milk. Cook over medium heat until thick and smooth. Add butter and vanilla. pour into baked pie crust. Cover with meringue. Bake at 400° until meringue is golden brown.

Pie Crust and Meringue: see page 121

Yield: 1 pie

MOONLITE'S PEANUT BUTTER PIE

16 ounces cream cheese, softened
2 cups powdered sugar
1 cup plain peanut butter
16 ounces Cool Whip

Mix cream cheese, powdered sugar and peanut butter well in mixer. Stir in Cool Whip, beat until fluffy. Pour into a 9-inch graham cracker crust pie crust. Sprinkle with chopped pecans or chocolate chips. Makes three pies. These pies can be frozen.

Graham Cracker Pie Crust: see page 120

Yield: 3 pies

Check this one out on our buffet. We now use the Chocolate Pie Crust recipe on page 120, but if you are in a hurry, you can use a purchased pie crust.

CATHERINE'S CHESS PIE

6 eggs
1 cup milk
½ cup corn starch
3 cups sugar
½ cup melted butter
2 tablespoons vanilla

Mix all ingredients together. Pour into an unbaked pie crust. Bake 10 minutes at 425°. Reduce heat to 350° and bake for about 30 minutes or until firm.

Pie Crust: see page 121

Yield: 1 pie

CHESS PIE

4 egg yolks
2 cups sugar, minus 4 tablespoons
1 cup cream
⅔ cup melted butter
1 teaspoon vanilla
2 rounded tablespoons flour

Beat together egg yolks, sugar, and flour. Add cream, vanilla and butter. Stir until well blended. Pour into unbaked pie crust. Bake at 375° until well done.

Pie Crust: see page 121

Yield: 1 pie

Aunt Nancy's Chess Pie

3 eggs, well beaten
1½ cups sugar
1 stick butter, minus 1 tablespoon
1 teaspoon vanilla
2 tablespoons vinegar

Melt butter. Mix all ingredients together. Pour into unbaked pie crusts and bake at 375° until done.

Aunt Nancy Tongate says that chess pie did not have cream added. Transparent pie had cream; chess pie had vinegar.

Pie Crust: see page 121

Yield: 1 pie

Transparent Pie

3 egg yolks, beaten
5 tablespoons cream
2 tablespoons butter or margarine
1 cup sugar
1 teaspoon vanilla

Mix (or work) room temperature butter into sugar. Add egg yolks, cream and vanilla. Pour into 9-inch unbaked pie crust and bake at 375° for about 30 minutes or until firm and light tan. This pie is very rich and so it shouldn't be too thick.

Pie Crust: see page 121

Yield: 1 pie

Chocolate Pie

1½ cups sugar

3 cups milk

⅓ cup cocoa

½ cup cornstarch

6 egg yolks, (save egg whites for meringue)

1 teaspoon vanilla

1 tablespoon butter

½ teaspoon salt

Mix together cocoa, sugar, salt and cornstarch. Add to milk and beaten egg yolks. Cook over medium heat until smooth and thick. Add vanilla. Pour into two baked pie crusts. Top with meringue and bake at 400° until brown.

Pie Crust and Meringue: see page 121

Yield: 2 Pies

Moonlite's Chocolate Pie has won blue ribbons at the Kentucky State Fair.

CHOCOLATE FUDGE PECAN PIE

1 cup sugar
½ stick butter or margarine
½ cup flour
1 cup pecans
1 cup chocolate chips
2 eggs, slightly beaten
1 tablespoon vanilla
1 pie crust, unbaked

Combine sugar, eggs, margarine, vanilla and flour in large mixing bowl. Blend well. Add chocolate chips and pecans. Mix well and pour into an unbaked pie crust. Bake at 375° for 30 minutes.

Pie Crust: see page 121

Yield: 1 pie

Chocolate Fudge Pecan Pie has become very popular in our Catering Department.

COCONUT PIE

1 cup sugar
½ cup cornstarch
3 cups milk
6 egg yolks (save whites for meringue)
½ teaspoon salt
1 teaspoon vanilla
1 cup coconut
1 tablespoon butter
Optional yellow food color
2 baked pie crusts

Mix sugar and cornstarch well in saucepan. Add milk and beaten egg yolks. Cook until thick, stirring constantly. Add butter, salt and vanilla. Drop 1 or 2 of yellow food color. Fold in coconut. Pour into two baked pie crusts. Top with meringue. Sprinkle with coconut and bake at 400° until coconut is brown.

Pie Crust and Meringue: see page 121

Yield: 2 pies

Moonlite's Coconut Pie has won blue ribbons at the Kentucky State Fair.

LEMON ICE BOX PIE

1 can Eagle Brand Milk
2 egg yolks, beaten
⅓ cup lemon juice

Mix and pour into baked Graham Cracker Pie Crust. Top with meringue and bake until brown.

Graham Cracker Pie Crust: see page 120
Meringue: see page 121

Yield: 1 pie

This recipe is so fast and easy. It's great for when you want dessert in a hurry!

Aunt Nancy & Uncle Kirk Tongate with Pappy Bosley

LEMON PIE

3 tablespoons cornstarch
1¼ cups warm water
Juice of 2 lemons
1 cup sugar
1 tablespoon butter
½ teaspoon of lemon rind, grated
3 egg yolks, beaten

Mix together cornstarch and sugar. Add lemon juice and beaten egg yolks. Slowly pour water over this mixture. Place in double boiler and cook until thick, stirring constantly, let cool to room temperature and pour into baked pie crust. Top with meringue and bake at 400° until brown.

Pie Crust and Meringue: see page 121

Yield: 1 pie

PECAN PIE

2 cups sugar

2 cups white syrup

6 eggs, beaten

2 teaspoons vanilla

2 tablespoons butter, melted

¼ teaspoon salt

2 cups pecans

2 pie crusts, unbaked

Mix together sugar, syrup, eggs, vanilla, butter and salt. Pour into unbaked pie crusts. Top with pecans. Bake at 425° for 10 minutes. Reduce heat to 300° and bake for 45 minutes.

Pie Crust: see page 121

Yield: 2 pies

PUMPKIN PIE

2 cups pumpkin
½ can Pet Milk
3 eggs, beaten
1 teaspoon cinnamon
1 teaspoon nutmeg
1 cup sugar
1 teaspoon vanilla
½ level teaspoon salt

Mix together all ingredients. Pour into an uncooked pie crust. Bake at 375° for approximately 1 hour until set. To see if the pie is done, a knife blade inserted 1 inch from the edge should come out clean.

Pie Crust: see page 121

Yield: 1 pie

When serving this pie you can dress up the plate with caramel sauce and top with whipped cream and cinnamon.

Rhubarb Custard Pie

1 cup sugar

3 tablespoons flour

3 egg yolks, beaten

2½ cups rhubarb, diced

2 tablespoons margarine

¼ teaspoon salt

Juice of one lemon

Dice rhubarb into 9-inch unbaked pie crust. Sprinkle dry ingredients on top of rhubarb. Add lemon juice then pour egg yolks over all. Add diced margarine. Bake at 325° for about 55 minutes.

Pie Crust: see page 121

Yield: 1 pie

For a sugar-free pie you can substitute 1 cup Splenda®.

GRAHAM CRACKER PIE CRUST

2 cups crushed graham crackers
½ cup melted butter
1 tablespoon flour

Mix together all ingredients. Press into pie pan. Bake until lightly brown.

Yield: 1 pie crust

CHOCOLATE PIE CRUST

2 cups crushed Oreo Cookies
½ cup melted butter
1 tablespoon flour

Mix together all ingredients. Press into pie pan. Bake at 350° for 10 minutes.

Yield: 1 pie crust

PIE CRUST

1½ cups self-rising flour
¼ cup ice cold water
½ cup Crisco
Extra flour for rolling out

Mix all ingredients well and chill for 8 hours or overnight. Roll out thin and place in a pie pan, pressing gently into the bottom of pie pan. Bake about 10 – 12 minutes at 450° or until brown. When baking, place an empty pie pan in the lining of the crust so it will not puff up.

Yield: 2 pie crusts

MERINGUE

1 cup egg whites
⅛ cup stabilizer
Enough water to make a medium paste
½ cup sugar

Put stabilizer in a small bowl. Add enough water to make a medium paste. Let stand 10 minutes to obtain maximum absorption. Put egg whites in a bowl and beat until a foam begins to form, then add stabilizer paste. Continue beating egg whites while slowly adding granulated sugar.

Continue whipping until stiff peaks form. Top pies and brown in a 400° oven.

Yield: 2 pies

You can purchase stabilizer at Moonlite. Using stabilizer keeps your meringue from "weeping".

Notes: Some things Grandmother Osborne taught us:

1. 1 cup light Corn syrup can be made by boiling together 1½ cup sugar and ⅓ cup water to syrup consistency. Using the same recipe but substitute dark brown sugar to make dark corn syrup.

2. Dark corn syrup can be substituted for Molasses, but your flavor will be milder.

3. You can make 1 cup of powdered sugar by using ⅞ cup granulated sugar and 1 tablespoon corn starch processed to a fine powder in a blender.

Desserts

Moonlite's Fruit Cobbler, page 124

MOONLITE'S FRUIT COBBLER

Photograph on page 123

Dough for Cobbler

3 cups self-rising flour
¾ cup Crisco shortening
¾ cup ice water (approximately)

Mix flour and Crisco with a fork or with fingers. Add water to right texture — not too sticky. Roll out mixture on wax paper, about ¼ inch thick. Turn into baking dish. Add filling. Fold remaining dough over the top of fruit filling and brush with melted butter. Bake at 350° for approximately 30 – 40 minutes or until brown. Sprinkle lightly with sugar and serve.

Fruit Filling

Apples:

4 cups frozen apples
1 cup sugar
½ cup clear gel
pinch of salt
½ teaspoon cinnamon

Peaches:

6 cups frozen peaches
1½ cups sugar
⅓ cup clear gel
⅔ cup water

(Continued)

(Fruit Filling continued)

Blackberries:

6 cups frozen blackberries
1 cup sugar
⅓ cup clear gel
⅔ cup water

Cherries:

6 cups frozen cherries
1 cup sugar
⅓ cup clear gel
⅔ cup water
Dash of red food coloring

Bring slightly thawed fruit to a full boil. Combine all other ingredients thoroughly in a separate bowl. Add to boiling fruit, stirring constantly. Cook 10 minutes.

Yield: One 5-Pound Cobbler

BAKED APPLES

1 (2 pound) package frozen apples, or 4 cups sliced
   apples
1½ tablespoons sugar
1 tablespoon butter
Pinch cinnamon
¼ teaspoon vanilla

Combine all ingredients except vanilla. Bake at 350° until tender, then add vanilla, stir and garnish with a light sprinkle of cinnamon.

Yield: 8 servings

WHOLE BAKED APPLES

6 fresh apples
Butter
Cinnamon
Salt

Core 6 fresh apples. Fill each with a dab of butter, a dash of cinnamon and a pinch of salt. Bake at 350° until tender.

Yield: 6 Servings

APRICOT BALLS CANDY

1 cup dried apricots
1 cup shredded coconut
¼ teaspoon grated orange rind
1 teaspoon grated lemon rind
1 tablespoon lemon juice
Granulated sugar
¼ cup powdered sugar

Put apricot and coconut through blender to chop fine. Mix in powdered sugar, rind, and lemon juice. Form into small balls. Roll into granulated sugar. Let ripen in the refrigerator at least one day before serving.

Yield: 2 dozen

AMBROSIA

A Bosley Christmas dessert since the early 1900's

3 cups orange sections, cut bite-size
1 cup fresh grated coconut
2 tablespoons sugar
½ cup cream
2 tablespoons powdered sugar

Combine orange sections, coconut and sugar. Whip the cream. Add 2 tablespoons powdered sugar. Fold into fruit mixture. Refrigerate.

Yield: 8 servings

Hugh & Catherine Bosley ca 1940.

Pat's Banana Foster

4 bananas, split and cut in half
½ cup butter
1 cup brown sugar
Dash cinnamon
1 shot Kirsh
1 shot rum
1 shot Cream of Banana
1 shot Triple Sec

Melt butter and brown sugar, stirring over heat. Add bananas. Add liquor. Ignite this mixture with a match. Fire will burn itself out. Add cinnamon. Serve immediately over ice cream.

BANANA PUDDING

2 or 3 bananas
1 cup sugar
½ cup cornstarch
3 cups milk
6 egg yolks (save egg whites for meringue)
½ teaspoon salt
1 teaspoon vanilla
1 tablespoon butter
8 ounces of Graham Crackers

Mix sugar and cornstarch well in saucepan. Add milk and beaten egg yolks. Cook until thick, stirring constantly. Add butter, salt and vanilla.

Layer 8 ounce Graham Crackers, filling and 2 or 3 bananas in a baking dish – a loaf pan is good. Top with meringue and brown.

Meringue: see page 121

Yield: 12 servings

Caramels

1 cup sugar
1 cup corn syrup
1½ cups cream
1 teaspoon vanilla
pinch of salt

Mix together sugar, syrup, salt and ½ cup of cream, stirring constantly. Let this come to a boil. Add ½ cup cream. Cook until this forms a soft ball when a small amount is dropped into a cup of cold water. Add remaining cream. Cook until hard ball stage is reached. Remove from heat. Add vanilla. Pour into greased pan.

Store caramels in a tin box in the refrigerator or another cool place.

"Great Grandmother used old metal ice trays for her caramels, Catherine recalls, "after the candy got hard, we'd cut it up into small pieces like kraft caramels and wrap each in wax paper. This is a good job for any small children that happen to be standing around.

Lucille's Caramel Recipe

2 cups sugar
2 cups white syrup
1 cup Pet Milk
½ stick butter

Mix all ingredients in a saucepan. Cook to a hardball stage. Add a teaspoon of vanilla and finish as above.

POPCORN BALLS

1 cup popping corn
1 cup brown sugar
½ cup molasses
¼ cup water
½ tablespoon vinegar
1 tablespoon butter
¼ teaspoon salt
2 cups peanuts, shelled and roasted

Pop the corn. Boil sugar, molasses and water until hardball is formed when tested in cold water. Hard ball is 280° on a candy thermometer. Add vinegar, butter and salt. Mix with popcorn and roasted peanuts. Butter your hands. Shape into balls, or spread onto cookie sheet and bake in the oven at 350° for a few minutes. Remove immediately from cookie sheet. Store in an airtight container.

Yield: 1 dozen fist sized balls

An old fashioned holiday treat. Aunt Nancy always had her nieces and nephews help her. If you do not have molasses, you can substitute dark corn syrup.

MOONLITE DELIGHT

1 can peaches
Prepared Dream Whip or Cool Whip
Handful chopped pecans

Drain 1 can peaches. Smoosh up with fingers. Fold in enough whipped cream to form a creamy consistency. Throw in handful of the chopped pecans and a few Maraschino cherries if you have them. Serve in pretty glass bowl.

This is a recipe that young children can make. Moretta lets her four-year old grandson make this by himself.

The Bosley Family in 2001
Front row: Pappy, Catherine and Janet Bosley Howard.
Back Row: Benny, Fred and Kenny

PEANUT BUTTER COOKIES

1 cup brown sugar
1 cup white syrup
½ cup shortening
2 eggs
1 cup peanut butter
2½ cups self-rising flour, sifted
1 teaspoon vanilla

Cream sugar, syrup and shortening. Add eggs and peanut butter. Add flour and vanilla. Roll into balls. Place onto greased cookie sheet, flatten with fork dipped in sugar, making crisscross pattern. Bake 10 minutes at 350°.

This family cookie recipe has been used in our Catering Department for many years, and is a favorite of Paige Bosley.

GRANDMOTHER OSBORNE'S TAFFY

2 cups sugar

1 cup water

2 tablespoons vinegar

1 teaspoon vanilla

1 lump butter, the size of a walnut

Mix sugar, water, vinegar and butter in heavy saucepan. Do not stir while cooking. Cook over medium heat until syrup spins a thread. Test this by dropping a spoonful of syrup into cold cup of water. If it is hard enough to crackle when hit on the side of the cup, it is done.

Pour into buttered platter. Do not scrape the saucepan. Cool until you can handle it. Add the vanilla. Butter your hands and pull by stretching it out and pulling ends together until it turns white. For variety, add food color for the holidays.

When it starts getting too hard to pull, stretch out as long and thin as you wish and cut into one inch pieces. Store in air tight container in cool area or refrigerator.

The Bosley grandchildren enjoy pulling this taffy.

Sunshine Loaf (Seafoam)

2 cups white sugar
2 cups brown sugar
1 cup white syrup
1 cup water

Stir only until dissolved. Cook until you have a workable ball (that is, when a few drops are dropped into cold water).

In another pan:

1 cup brown sugar
½ cup water

Cook this until it spins a thread (or until it will crack on a cup). To test this, take a teaspoon half full and place in a cup of cold water. If it forms a hard ball that will crack on the side of a cup, it is done. If the ball is too soft, cook a while longer. Or hold the spoon over the mixture and pour. If it spins a thread it is ready.

Beat three egg whites while syrup is cooking. Add a pinch of salt (1/3 teaspoon). Beat in first mixture, then second mixture. add one teaspoon of vanilla and one cup of chopped nuts. Beat until stiff (it will lose its glossy look). Pour into greased pan or cake dish.

Once cool, cut into squares and coat with chocolate dip (see next page) top with a pecan half. Place on waxed paper until set.

Catherine says, "great grandmother is the only person I've ever known who could make this candy. I attempt to make it every christmas. It never turns out as good as hers. If the candy didn't get hard, she'd stick it in the oven (coal stove) so she could beat it again. Then she would stand on the back porch in the freezing weather and beat it by hand to help cool it. The next day she would cut the candy into squares and dip it in chocolate.

CHOCOLATE DIP
For Sunshine Loaf

Great Grandmother would use anything she could find; semi-sweet chocolate chips or pure chocolate blocks, or a mixture of the two.

Melt the chocolate in a double boiler on top of the stove. Add a piece of paraffin wax to make it shine and harden quicker. Remove from the stove, leaving the chocolate in the hot water. Use toothpicks to dip the candy squares. Place each on wax paper and top with a pecan half while the chocolate is still soft. Store in a cool place.

"This is the most delicious candy in the world and everyone should try it. Last Christmas I set aside an evening and tackled it for the tenth time. It was far into the night (2 a.m.) when it was finished. My feet were sticking to the floor; my hands stuck to the refrigerator door. There was as much candy on me as there was on the dish. Nevertheless, we had our seafoam for Christmas and even packed a few small boxes for gifts. Maybe next Christmas I'll have better luck and it will be just like mom's," says Catherine Bosley.

Grandmother Osborne setting a pan of Sunshine Loaf out to cool.

SPICE GUIDE

Spices	Salads	Meat & Poultry	Fish	Vegetables	Desserts
All Spice	Fruit Salads especially peach & pineapple	Pot roast & roast duck, gravies, stew, corned or boiled beef	Use in marinade or water for boiling	Beets and tomato sauce	Puddings, mincemeat, pumpkin pie, fruitcake
Cayenne	Many Salads	Meat & gravies, chicken, stew, pizza, spaghetti	All fish & seafood	Vegetables and sauces	Usually not used in desserts
Cinnamon	Fruit Salads	Tomato-meat sauces	Usually not used with fish	Mashed sweet potatoes	Puddings, baked goods, fruit and chocolate desserts
Chili	Avocado & egg salad	Beef & lamb stew, chicken fricassee, hamburgers, meat loaf, chili con carne	Broiled fillets; all fish, cocktail sauces	Corn	Usually not used in desserts
Cloves	Usually not used in salads	Pot roast, lamb & beef stews, ham, pork roast, tongue, corn & boiled beef	Usually not used with fish	Many vegetables, especially good in tomato	Fruit & chocolate desserts, baked goods, mince-meat, fruitcake
Curry	Chicken or egg salads	Meat & poultry, curries, lamb & beef stew, veal, fried & roast chicken, hamburgers	Fish curries, clam & fish chowders, shrimp	vegetables and sauces, creamed onion, rice, buttered cabbage	Usually not used in desserts
Ginger	Fruit salads	Pot roast, creamed or roast chicken	Sauces for fish	Squash	Any fruit dessert, gingerbread, cookies, pumpkin pie
Mace	Fruit salads	Poultry sauces & stuffing, chicken pie, gravies	Almost all fish & fish sauces	Potatoes	Fruit & chocolate desserts, pound cake, gingerbread
Mustard	Potato & egg salads, salad dressings	Ham gravies	Fish sauces	Vegetable sauces & dressing, boiled cabbage, sauerkraut	Usually not used in desserts
Nutmeg	Fruit salads & dressings	Chicken soup & stews	Creamed oysters	Most vegetables & vegetable sauces	Most fruit desserts, pud-dings & custard, doughnuts & baked goods
Paprika	Most salads & salad dressings	Meat, chicken, gravies	All fish	All vegetables & vegetable sauces	Usually not used in desserts
Pepper	Any vegetables, meat, poultry or fish salads	All meat & poultry dishes, gravies & sauces	All fish & fish sauces	All vegetables & vegetable sauces	Usually not used in desserts
Saffron	Usually not used in salads	Chicken dishes	Some fish dishes	Add to water when cooking rice	Some fancy rolls & biscuits
Turmeric	Salads & salad dressings	Meat dishes	Fish, seafood & fish sauces	Corn relish	Usually not used in desserts

Recipe Index

Acknowledgements

We would like to acknowledge the following members of the Moonlite family and wish to thank them for their contributions to this cookbook.

Catherine Bosley
Paulette Osborne
Nancy Tongate
Hugh B. "Pappy" Bosley
Janet Howard
Fred Bosley
Beverly Bosley
Hugh B. "Benny" Bosley
Sue Bosley
Kenneth Bosley
Moretta Bosley
Jeannie Bosley Heath
Lucille Tong
Martha Murray
Chris Bosley
Patrick Bosley

Thank you to the many others whose recipes have been recorded and handed down without acknowledgement.

A special thank you must be given to Mrs. Catherine Bosley and to her mother, Mrs. Pauline Osborne. Without their many years of preparing a number of these recipes, this cookbook would not be complete. To these two marvelous ladies we are forever grateful.

Order Form

Use the order form below or visit our website at www.moonlite.com

---

You may order as many copies of our cookbook as you wish for the regular price plus postage and packing per book ordered. Mail to:

Moonlite Bar-B-Q Inn, Inc.
2840 W. Parrish Avenue
Owensboro, Kentucky 42301

Please mail _____ copies of your cookbook @ $21.95 per book ordered, price includes postage and handling.

Mail Books to:
Name _____

Address _____

City, State, Zip _____

You may order as many copies of our cookbook as you wish for the regular price plus postage and packing per book ordered. Mail to:

Moonlite Bar-B-Q Inn, Inc.
2840 W. Parrish Avenue
Owensboro, Kentucky 42301

Please mail _____ copies of your cookbook @ $21.95 per book ordered, price includes postage and handling.

Mail Books to:
Name _____

Address _____

City, State, Zip _____

Moonlite Bar-B-Q Inn, Inc.
Phone: 270-684-8143 • 800-322-8989 • Fax: 270-684-8105
Mail Order Office Hours 9am to 4pm Monday — Friday
email: help@moonlite.com